TEACH FOR TODAY
or
TRAIN FOR TOMORROW

TEACH FOR TODAY
or
TRAIN FOR TOMORROW

Martha A. Harper

Archway Publishing books may be ordered through booksellers or by contacting:

Archway Publishing
1663 Liberty Drive
Bloomington, IN 47403
www.archwaypublishing.com
1 (888) 242-5904

ISBN: 978-1-4808-3314-2 (sc)
ISBN: 978-1-4808-3315-9 (e)

Library of Congress Control Number: 2016910204

Print information available on the last page.

Archway Publishing rev. date: 6/27/2016

Dedication

This book and all the time, thoughts, and preparation involved in its development is dedicated to Timothy Mason, a very driven man who loves to dance, loves to win (former champion in International Standard with wife, Michele), but more importantly loves to teach. He now considers his professional priority to be coaching his staff and preparing them for daily quality dance instruction. Timothy accepted me as a student, an "unknown," introducing me to International Standard and competing with me at a national level, as well as introducing me to the concept of dance imagery. Watching and listening to him during our lessons and instructing his staff, he truly is a dancer, coach, judge, and trainer who has a vision to share his heart and his talent.

When you dance...

❧ *music touches your hearts,*

❧ *hearts stir your spirits,*

❧ *your spirits connect,*

❧ *joy is expressed in movement...*

Foreword By Arunas Bizokas

Master's in Education, Lithuanian Sports University, Kaunas, Lithuania; Professional International Standard World Champion; United States Terpsichore Association Member Certifications: International Standard, American Ballroom, International Latin, Theatre Arts.

Communication is primary to dancing, especially if information is to be effectively transferred from one person to another. When a student comes to me for lessons communication is the first thing on our agenda, even before dancing. You have to know and understand the other person to maximize their learning. We respect your technical dance education and experience. This training program is about empowering you as a professional to fine tune your teaching methods and then to pass them on to other developing professionals. This will ultimately strengthen the intake and performance of new dance students. In combination with your natural talent, technical skills, and current teaching resources, I feel this program will yield a significant return on your time investment for you personally, and for the instructors and students you connect with for the future.

Arunas Bizokas

Preface

International dance communities have a deep pool of resources to expand markets around the globe. I am eager to be a part of the outreach and contribute a training tool for your consideration. Let's toss this pebble into the pool and watch for the continuing rippling effect it could have on tomorrow's instructors. If you teach a person a designated syllabus, it may stop there. If you train a person to secure the information then share the syllabus with another through creative instructional processes, who shares it with another, who shares it with another, then we're looking at quality dance instruction multiplying into lots of tomorrows. From a business standpoint, this program has potential to impact studio revenue by a) increasing retention of current students through stronger instructional delivery, b) improving marketability to potential students, and additionally c) stabilizing your employee base with long term instructors, reducing hiring and training cost. Many have formal certification for technical dance instruction. My contribution is a Master's degree in Education Leadership and experience working with people who have specialized skill sets to enhance their instructional delivery. I have 18 years performing and competing in American Smooth, Rhythm, Latin and International Standard. This program is designed for qualified and experienced dance professionals to fine tune their instructional skills, multiplying their professional and creative expertise to other instructors. Please take a look -

Martha

Program Description

This program is for experienced dance professionals interested in strengthening their instructional skills. It includes some self-evaluation of commitment to teaching, willingness to learn, mental creativity with ability to demonstrate, and communication skills to effectively share with new instructors as well as amateur students.

There is one Latin exercise and the other International Standard to measure awareness of learning methods to include reading, hearing, seeing, doing. The program is interactive to promote sharing of instructional practices. You have two dance imagery series to stir inner creativity and benefit from input of your dance professional peers. It is refreshing to acquire new teaching tools and sharpen those you currently use.

You live to dance! When the music starts your feet and body go in motion. Everybody gets a chance to partner and practice what has been shared. Be ready; we open the floor to perform but also to critique. Eager to listen and learn, to grow and glow? We invite you to try the program.

Acknowledgment

First, thanks to my family for their endurance of my passion for dance; to Ari, John, Chandler and Jack heart smiles for fun and friendship shared in the photo shoot; grace and honor to Julia for being the example of elegance and humility in coaching as well as performing; my deepest appreciation to Vasiliy and Marina for their desire to train students to be the best they can be; to "Mr. K" who has intermittently shown up throughout my eighteen years of dance always expressing kindness with a smile; to Brent for his gentle patience in starting me on this journey; to Jim for "catching" me in difficult times to keep me on the dance floor; to Sandy and Joyce for teaching me key elements of appearance and confidence; to John for sharing his vision of perfection; to Sharon who has dressed me in such stunning fashion and offered support on every turn; to Sasha who by personal example taught me sacrifice and drive to keep dancing; to Magdalena and Sven for trusting me in our corporate educational endeavors; to Colin for his respect of me as a person, introducing me to the global arenas of ballroom dancing; and ultimately my most special thanks to Arunas for his joy, his humility, his inner strength of character, and his sensitivity to listen with his heart and share with me his desire and vision for giving to others.

Contents

Facilitator: _____   **Professionals: 6 Pairs**

Session 1, Class A   Taste of the Journey

Latin Presentation - "Call of the Wild: View into Africa"

Learning Processes: What did you notice first or will remember tomorrow?

- ❖ Title (Reading):

- ❖ Music (Hearing):

- ❖ Appearance (Seeing):

- ❖ Choreography (Doing):

We'll come back to this . . .

Are You . . .

Committed? Teachable? Creative? Communicative?

Learning is all about **Attitude**. If you are eager to take something new home with you, you'll do it. You'll listen a little closer, watch for the unexpected, or try a different method. You may be interested in taking personal notes. Blank pages throughout the book are provided for this purpose. As the program progresses consider improvements in your instructional practices; recognize and remember what they are. As you implement new training programs, these types of memory excerpts could be helpful to your trainees. Also, be open to give and receive comments to diversify the learning resources of everyone here. Asking questions and sharing ideas are exciting, entertaining and creative parts of learning.

Attitude: *Committed*

Please share with the group 1) why you decided to come and 2) do you have an instructional area you want to improve.

Selection Considerations for this Program:

- ➤ Do you have a commitment for continuous development?
- ➤ Are you willing to sacrifice to grow?
- ➤ Are you consistent in attitude and behavior as you teach?
- ➤ Are you responsible to follow up for you and your students?

Why and when did you choose to start a career in dancing?

What would be the fulfillment of your dance pursuits?

Describe your most effective coach/instructor.

What might be your greatest challenge in this program?

What is your objective in completing this program?

Currently, how do you rate yourself? (1 is low - 5 is high)

- ↯ Creative _____
- ↯ Disciplined _____
- ↯ Perceptive _____
- ↯ Communicator _____

Partnership

What do you have in mind to find the right partner, or more importantly, to be the right partner? Addressed here are aspects of personal and social concern.

Perseverance – through good times and bad, willing to push through unexpected difficulties to achieve long range goals; flexible to adjust to any challenge.

Attitude – consistently projecting positive intent; eager to see the best in any person or circumstance; willing to forgive and move forward.

Realistic – ability to maintain clarity in communication and decision making; can take a look at the "big picture" of a situation; least likely to become defensive and will promote honesty.

Teachable – open to learn and to grow; listens to suggestions, explores new options; sharpens skills daily to improve dancing and partnership.

Neutral – equalizes emotions when faced with different opinion; may have a strong personality or convictions yet self-image is not threatened; practices self-control, respects input of others.

Energetic – presents a daily upbeat demeanor (though not overpowering); enjoys fun and laughter in practice, performance and competition; contributes whatever is required to fine tune the partnership.

Responsible – both personally and professionally able to invest and maintain in the areas of communication, preparation, finances and health.

Session 1, Class B

Attitude: *Teachable*

What is your Primary Learning Style? Let's get everyone's feedback from the demonstration. This might give us a hint as to what learning style is most effective for your intake and retention. Did the title draw your interest? (reading) Did you quickly lock into the music? (hearing) Did the dancers' appearance catch your eye? (seeing) Did you focus on their choreography? (doing)

Latin Presentation: "Call of the Wild: View into Africa"

Professionals: Feed It Back

- ❖ Title (Reading):

- ❖ Music (Hearing):

- ❖ Appearance (Seeing):

- ❖ Choreography (Doing):

Attitude: *Creative* - Dance Imagery

Stand up and find some space to move. As the imagery is read, demonstrate it out –

"Nature's Warm-Up"

If I plant my feet to the ground, I will stretch tall and strong, like a tree reaching for the sun.

🖑 **Instruction:** Keep feet to the floor to maintain balance and posture for all movement originates from your core.

Professionals: What are your ideas?

Frame / Foundation –

Energy -

Core –

If I look to the moon and the stars, I will sparkle like starlight in the night sky.

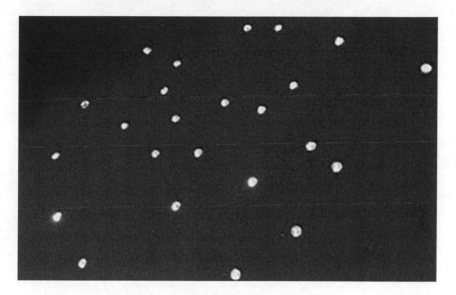

🕻 **Instruction:** Head and eyes up with the attitude that you have something special to share with the audience.

Professionals: What are your ideas?

Presentation –

Attitude –

Facial / body expression-

If I embrace the wind, I will move across the dance floor like a bird in flight.

🦶 **Instruction:** Free movement, seamless; stay focused and balanced whether hovering, swaying or elevating.

Professionals: What are your ideas?

Owning the floor –

Extension –

Musicality -

**If I reach for the hearts of the audience, I will
pull them close, then share them with you.**

🎵 **Instruction:** Dance to express joy with the audience and with
your partner.

Professionals: What are your ideas?

Expressions of face and body –

Unity with partner –

Audience contact -

Session 1, Class C

Attitude: *Communicative* - Instructional Skills

Break into three Teams:

- Team A: Couples 1 & 2
- Team B: Couples 3 & 4
- Team C: Couples 5 & 6

Couples 2 – 4 - 6 teach your own dance pattern to your team members, Couples 1 – 3 - 5; remember to watch and listen for their primary learning tools. Did you bring your music? Couples 1 – 3 – 5 then perform for the group what they learned.

Responding to the questions below, Couples 1 – 3 – 5 measure the training effectiveness of their Team Members, Couples 2 – 4 –6.

Scoring: A-Highly Effective; B-Effective; C-Good; D-Fair

Question:

1. Committed to help you learn the pattern? Score: _____
2. Sensitive to your best learning process? Score: _____
3. Creative in their instructional delivery? Score: _____

Learning processes used most often in their instruction?

Reading – Hearing – Seeing – Doing

May be good communicators; how to improve?

Attitude: *Communicative* – Instructional skills (continued)

The 6 couples reconvene and switch roles: Couples 1–3–5 now teach your pattern to Couples 2 – 4 – 6.

Stay in your three teams:

- Team A: Couples 1 & 2
- Team B: Couples 3 & 4
- Team C: Couples 5 & 6

Couples 1 – 3 - 5 teach your own dance pattern to your team members, Couples 2 – 4 - 6; remember to watch and listen for their primary learning tools. Did you bring your music? Couples 2 – 4 – 6 then perform for the group what they learned.

The same Couples 2 – 4 – 6 next use the evaluation chart below to measure the training effectiveness of their team members, Couples 1 – 3 – 5.

Scoring: A-Highly Effective; B-Effective; C-Good; D-Fair

Question:

1. Committed to help you learn the pattern? Score: _____
2. Sensitive to your best learning process? Score: _____
3. Creative in their instructional delivery? Score: _____

Learning processes used most often in their instruction?

Reading – Hearing – Seeing - Doing

May be good communicators; how to improve?

Session 1, Class D - Recap

Attitude: Committed   Teachable   Creative   Communicative

Teachable: Reading? Hearing? Seeing? Doing?

Creative: Dance Imagery

Communicative: Do you have to repeat instruction often?

Self – Evaluation:

How could I be better prepared to train a new professional?

Anything in the article "Partnership" that strikes home?

What instructional areas do I need to work on?

Am I sensitive to identify interests of my student?

Am I able to spontaneously create dance imagery?

Article - Learning Processes: "Let's try that again . . ."

"I need to study the syllabus again." (Reading) "Could you repeat that?" (Hearing) "Please show me my part again." (Seeing) "Let's try it in partner; I need to dance it for myself." (Doing)

Most individuals have a primary learning process of which four examples are given above. While working on my Educational degree, a professor missed detailing one of his lecture points on the board. I asked him to write it out. He commented, "Martha, I forgot one of your primary learning processes is visual." This motivated me to identify a student's most effective learning process and structure my lessons accordingly. In ballroom dancing, I realized how often I asked my instructor to demonstrate my part (seeing). I also realized I needed the other three (hearing, reading, and doing) to maintain a balanced educational track. So whether you're teaching an individual or group, it is good to use all four.

Reading To see the technical description in print and reading through it provides continuity and affirms the verbal. It clarifies the detail. Syllabuses are publicly available in most studios and on the internet. It is helpful if the instructor reviews the written instructions before a lesson. Ballroom and Latin dancing are frequent topics of discussion outside the studio so students compare information. Often students take from several instructors in different studios so they will be looking for consistency in their written material. As a student becomes more committed and desires to improve, they may take notes after each lesson. This is another avenue of learning which assists the student by reading their personal references in their own handwriting.

Hearing Some people hear information once, process it and play it back with minimal error. It also helps if the instructor is clear with their verbal description of pattern and technique. If there is a language difference or the instructor is a new professional, it might

help if they studied a little more in advance of each lesson or asked another professional for clarity. It is a plus if the instructor and student agree to question when there is a concern with the language exchange. A major part of hearing is also the music. Teaching musicality is sometimes difficult, but listening to the music can provide understanding to the movement. It provides a framework for the dance itself. To me it is like "connecting the dots" and getting a feel for how the many parts come together.

Seeing. When watching a lesson demonstration, I am looking for execution of feet interwoven with body movement. It helps me to see it several times, and I appreciate an instructor who switches roles to show me my steps before dancing as partners. A person who is a visual learner takes mental notes of what they see, then plays it back in memory for improved understanding, practice, and retention. I take note when I see an instructor preparing for a lesson and dancing their steps in front of a mirror. They need to see what the student sees when they verbalize and demonstrate the steps / choreography.

Doing Clearly doing is a required element of learning as you need to practice what you have learned. In an eagerness to respond to the music, exemplify their knowledge or skill, or the sheer creative excitement of trying something new, a student may start doing before their process of learning has developed. Sometimes a student is a little fearful of doing it wrong and the instructor has to encourage them to just step out and try it. This usually helps open them up to improve and advance their learning options.

Learning is fun and exciting! I love Hearing a new idea, a new step. Then Reading about it increases my interest and understanding. Seeing it in motion brings it to a whole new reality and expectation. Then actually Doing it, and doing it right, is an ultimate pleasure and joy which both the student and the instructor share!

TEACH FOR TODAY
OR
TRAIN FOR TOMORROW
Session 2 of 2

Session 2, Class A   Personal Development, Refresh

Time Warp! What has happened since we last saw each other?

1. What is different in your own learning process and intake?
2. How has your awareness improved of a student's learning processes?
3. To what degree has your creativity developed?
4. What have you found to be your communication keys?

Refresh

➢ **Committed** - to multiplying out quality dance instruction
➢ **Teachable** - continuous self-improvement to increase personal training effectiveness
➢ **Creative** - greater awareness of student interest, quicker visual images to improve their understanding
➢ **Communicative** - repeating familiar phrases for retention, more descriptive for student's understanding

Special things I want to remember:

Session 2, Class B

Attitude: *Creativity* (additional dance imagery)

"A Walk Through The Kingdom"

🦅 **Instruction:** Head up, shoulders back; smile. Your kingdom is the dance floor, and your subjects are your audience.

Professionals: What are your ideas?

Presentation -

Partner Connection -

Form -

It takes two . . . To Honor

🌢 **Instruction:** Honor, respect, communication; for the purpose of this time and to please your audience, you belong to each other and consider one another as you move.

Professionals: What are your ideas?

Gentleman frames the lady; knows his direction

Lady connects to support; follows his lead

Power of a rocket boost upward –

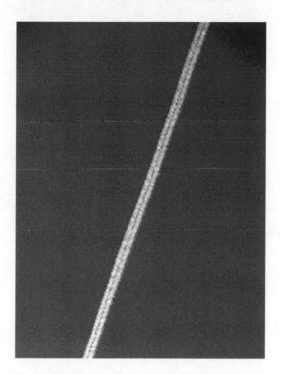

🎗 **Instruction:** Extension - Eyes, energy, and body movement arch upward. Movement - Seamless and connected from one pattern to another.

Professionals: What are your ideas?

Body extension -

Exchange of energy -

Continuous movement -

To walk along the seashore,
rolling with the waves in the sand –

🍂 **Instruction:** Foot movement - Roll forward, heel to toe – roll backward, toe to heel; continuous and controlled, reaching into the floor as you "mold" your feet in the sand.

Professionals: What are your ideas?

Foot and leg, coordinated timely movement -

Heel leads -

Extension and control -

To sway in a gentle breeze through a meadow, or twist and turn through dips and hills.

🦶 **Instruction:** Body gently moves with the wind in swaying motion (Standard or Smooth); or through isolation and sharp footwork, moves in and around your partner (Latin and Rhythm).

Professionals: What are your ideas?

Rotation and Sway -

Isolation and arm styling -

Hips, arm, head coordination -

Session 2, Class C

Attitude: *Creativity* (spontaneous)

How fast do you think on your feet? Take your partner, spend 15 minutes to create your own dance imagery per items listed below. Every couple will have an opportunity to present your dance imagery to the group. Following each presentation, the floor is open for comments. Are they descriptive and clear? How could they improve their instruction?

Couple #1 - Contra body movement

Couple #2 – Heel Turn

Couple #3 - Isolation

Couple #4 – Samba Walk

Couple #5 – Cross Body Lead

Couple #6 – Frame set up

Building for Tomorrow

Teaching: You know what to teach, having syllabus certification. List dances to add to your certification or improve. When?

Challenging: You have awareness of improved learning skills. What instructional areas do you want to strengthen? How?

Correcting: You developed a sensitivity to identify growth areas. Improve evaluation skills and ways to encourage growth. Resources?

Training: You desire to help others fine tune their teaching skills. Who can assist you with communication skills to trainees/students?

Personal Objectives:

Our Last Reflection - International Standard Presentation

"Top of the Mountain: View of Austria"

Professionals: Feed It Back

- ❖ Title (Reading):

- ❖ Music (Hearing):

- ❖ Appearance (Seeing):

- ❖ Choreography (Doing):

Comments:

Facilitator Tips

Learning is positive anticipation; let your expression convey that.
Lay a solid foundation; know your material and stick to it.
Stay on your feet – Circle the room – Pause for Impact
Connect with trainees; ask questions to engage them. Keep them alert and involved.
Have positive closure to each question.
Laughter minimizes fear and conflict, and encourages learning.

Potential Issues: If a trainee is
- testing your authority – discuss after class; move on to next point,
- not understanding – let another clarify,
- hesitant to respond – suggest to discuss with partner.

Listen to them, take notes; make training relevant to their thoughts.
Stick to your outline; change application if needed to maintain interest.
Learning is a process: always build on the material; build "up" or "out".

Introduce the Program; Conduct the Program; Summarize the Program

Epilogue

At five I started dance lessons in ballet, tap and jazz. Later came square dancing and ballroom, both requiring a partner. There were some inactive periods, but six decades later I am still hungry to perform, compete and experience with my partner the opportunity to share with an audience the thrill of dance. Running from grade school to be on time for dance lessons, cramming my ballroom lessons between work and university classes, finishing my homework in the studio, and stretching my lunch "hour" from my job to get extra practice, please know this training program is more than an educational exercise for me.

A professional dancer may be proficient at performing, competing, choreographing, and/or teaching. Some dance for the fame, to supplement income, for the social aspect, or for the pleasure of teaching. If an instructor expresses interest in a training program, take time to hear what they're actually asking. Do they have a commitment and a vision for the long journey? Are they looking for a title or something to add to their credentials? If they really have a heart for the learning and the training, you'll know . . . and thank you for sharing *your* heart with us.